THROU

Poems of Beautiful Northeast Ohio

Edited by Floriana Hall
330-928-8492

Floriana102@aol.com
Www.expage.com/flossiesbooknook

Fifteen poets from Akron and surrounding areas met
At Taylor-Memorial Library since June 1999 to get
A book put together for your pleasure -
A book of places and memories to treasure,
A book we hope will please your fancy and lift your mood,
And for your perusal, we extend our gratitude..

The Poets

Printed by Pip Printing,
1127 Portage Trail,
Cuyahoga Falls, Ohio

THROUGH OUR EYES -
Poems of Beautiful Northeast Ohio

CONTENTS - LOCAL POETS

ANGELA BAKER

When I was born on the eastside of Cleveland, Ohio, my parents named me Angela Marie Musarra. Being born in America and having an Italian heritage has made me feel twice blessed: for I appreciate my roots, being free and loving people.

At the age of eight I experienced a call to serve God. Seventeen years later, I proclaimed the gospel through singing, poetry, writing testimonies in short story form, teaching Bible studies and speaking to women's groups and also becoming certified through the State of Ohio as a chaplain.

Among the biggest blessings in my life is sharing all this with my husband, three wonderful daughters, and our grandchildren.

The Bakers reside in Cuyahoga Falls.

I would like it to be said of the people I touch; that Angela Baker operates in mercy and is an encourager.......declaring the Hope I have in me.

1

As I walked north on 23rd Street in Cuyahoga Falls
everything became alive with sounds and colors.

AN EARLY SPRING WALK

The sweet song of spring birds fill the air with the sound
of their sweet concert.
My Best Friend walks with me
and we take in the beauty of His creation all around.
To see the budding leaves on each tree
reminds me of His love for me.
Life goes on...There's order and a special plan...
And...He holds me securely in His hand.
I enter the music of the day for He has clothed me with joy
As I lift to Him my praise.
Like the singing birds and the budding trees...
The love we share brings fulfillment and peace.

Of the sky overhead at daybreak:

BEAUTIFUL SUNRISE

A beautiful sunrise showed itself in view this day
Dressing in a gown of pretty pink array
Covering the earth in splendid display
Shrouding the darkness of night away.

ENTER THE DANCE, GIVE GOD A CHANCE

It was funny watching my umbrella dance
As it bounced with the wind up and down
I too entered into the rhythm of the dance
As my feet tried not to slip on the ground.

It was hard to smile, though I fought with the wind
It made me see life clear for awhile
There are times when the wind blows harder
And the rain clouds cover the sun...
But like magic, that very same wind
Will soon blow those rainclouds away.

So if the day starts out dreary
Try not to worry...
Look for the sun to shine today
Give God a chance to turn what seems so bad...
To a beautiful dance where your feet
Will walk steadfastly on His path
For He cares for you and me, too,
Because our lives are part of His plan.

So let's hold onto His Hand as we enter the dance
A better partner we could never have
For He knows each way to turn,
and He'll never lead us wrong
Even when the wind and the rain are strong
God is our trusted friend
Through the concert of our lives each day on.

FLORIANA BERDYCK HALL

Poet and Author Floriana Berdyck Hall, born Oct. 2, 1927 in Pittsburgh, Pa. Parents: Francis B. Berdyck and Floriana C. Schmitt. Family settled in Cuyahoga Falls, Ohio, on December 7, 1941. June 1945 graduate of Cuyahoga Falls High School, eleventh in class of 167. Wrote for CFHS newspaper, and solicited advertising while working after school. Attended Akron University Business School.

Private secretary to the Comptroller of The General Tire & Rubber Co. Worked for Chemical Workers Union, Akron Legal News; Summit County Courthouse.

Married to Robert E. Hall, World War 11 Veteran, since December 31, 1948, five children, nine grandchildren.

Member St. Martha Church since 1960, Sunday School teacher, Greeter, Lector, prayer groups. PTA Secretary, Jackson School, Akron Art Institute volunteer, CFHS Band Booster, Friends of Taylor Library.

Inspired in church to write LOVE NEVER DIES, first published poem which won Editor's Choice Award in The National Library of Poetry's Anthology 'Sea of Treasures.' Has had over 175 poems published in NLP's anthologies, and in various books and magazines in the United States and Great Britain, winning one 1st prize, four 3rd prizes, seven Editor's Choice Awards, and seven Honorable Mentions. Writes short stories, ten published. Writes poems on request.

Published two books: SMALL CHANGE, the true story of her life as a child during the Great Depression, which teaches children to appreciate what they have; and THE SANDS OF RHYME, easy to understand inspirational poetry. Both books sell at Borders and Barnes & Noble and on the internet.

DADDY WAS A BAD BOY , adult version of SMALL CHANGE will be on the market in the year 2000.

Floriana, is a Distinguished Member of ISP-NLP, Poet's League of Greater Cleveland, The Famous Poet's Society, and others.

Her priorities in life are God, family, friends, country, and helping others. Her motto is: "The secret of life is not to take it personally."

A TEEN'S VIEW OF AKRON IN 1941

When I first moved from the rolling hills of Pittsburgh to Akron
At the impressionable age of almost fourteen,
What first caught my eye was Main Street with its department stores -
Akron Dry Goods, Yeagers, Federmans, Polsky's, O'Neils,
Its many shops, restaurants and movie theaters -
Orpheum, Colonial, Strand, and Loews.
My brothers and I crossed the bridge to downtown
Passing St. Thomas Hospital from Penfield Ave. on down -
What a magnificent panoramic view, we were in awe,
A brand new city, we liked what we saw.
On Main Steet, we could walk to shop at any store
Or see a quarter movie, choices galore.
Lowe's theater was our favorite place to be,
The illusion of being in heaven came to me
While sitting in the balcony with stars twinkling in the sky
And 'Wild Oscar' playing the organ on a platform so high.
When we walked up the hill to Broadway Street,
Quaker Oats granary bins our eyes did meet,
Then St. Bernard's was an architectural attraction to behold,
The White Tower a stop as we strolled on our way
For a treat of a burger on a special day,
We thought Akron was the best town to know,
And beautiful Ohio the best state in the nation to grow.

BENJAMIN FRANKLIN GOODRICH
(1841-1888)

Benjamin Franklin Goodrich
Studied medicine in New York City,
However, he found his permanent niche
When he switched to the rubber industry.
He had confidence in rubber's future -
Bicycle tires made from latex pure -
the juice of a tree,
Moved to Akron, Ohio in 1870,
Founded the B. F. Goodrich Company
In the "Rubber Capital of the world"
Making tires, insulation, home and many other products,
Synthetics increased since World War II
At Goodrich, Goodyear, Firestone, General Tire, too.
Every company except Goodyear has left our city
What a loss and what a pity!
Empty buildings downtown became Canal Place
However, replacement can't compare
To Akron's former industrial pace.
And I imagine Ben would be turning over in his grave
If he could see the changes that have been made.

REJUVENATION

Charismatic Akron, pragmatic, aromatic
Rubber companies, industry flourishing
People working, systems working automatically,
Employment rate encouraging.

Slowly, surprisingly, deliberately,
Gallery of faces and factories move on
Leaving emptiness and hallowness behind,
Ultimately the people respond in kind.

The people are the city,
The arch of human society,
Everyone prepared to take the helm
Steering away from community anxiety.

Hostility, civility, creativity,
Government rising to the occasion
Exploring every possibility,
Work force part of the equation.

Like a colony of ants, group interests come first
Civilization downloading propriety and kindness
A revamped downtown proposal, diverse,
Renovating, rejuvenating, stimulating mindset.

Akron's past faded into oblivion
Sparking a new heritage revival
New metropolitan interests living on
Voted best in productive survival.

AKRON'S FIRST NIGHT

On New Year's Eve in forty-eight
Our wedding vows were spoken
What better way to celebrate anniversaries
Than Akron's First Night token.

Cold, crisp, stars in the evening sky
Not a sign of snow
Too windy for hot-air balloons to fly
But many other places to go.

Ballet in the Civic on stage
At the library, skits of favorite plays
John S. Knight Hall, lively bands
Inventure Place discoveries by hand.

Dinner in the Orangerie Mall
Talented voices blended in song,
Bussing to E.J. Thomas Hall
Symphony Orchestra enjoyed by throngs.

St. Bernards the subsequent stop
The most elaborate church downtown
Choirs of many different flocks
Dressed in suitable similar frocks.

Quaker Square shopping or browsing
Ensemble of music, soothing, blithe
No alcoholic beverages or carousing
On Akron's yearly family fun night.

Fireworks exploding, grand finale show
The fabulous Aero's Stadium, frozen toes
Midnight kisses start the New Year
Greeting the new millennium without fear.

THE UNIVERSITY OF AKRON

Part of Akron's illustrious history
Is its pride in its university,
A multicultural community -
Teachers, engineers, lawyers
Graduate, some cum laude, each year
Business majors, future leaders,
Speakers you may someday hear.
You can study most any course
To help you to succeed,
Grants and scholarships, available source
To cover necessities you need.
Professors who excel in subjects old and new,
Football, basketball, other sports
To participate or view,
E. J. Thomas Hall, on stage,
Akron Symphony orchestra, musical sage.
The University of Akron attracts scholars from every state
With high academic credentials
And educational opportunities first-rate.
When you are exploring colleges to attend,
Remember, Akron U. is just around the bend.

THE HIKING SPREE

There are many different trails
In Akron area's Metropolitan Parks,
We hike along them every fall
Sometimes even in the dark.

The first year earns a hiking stick
After walking eight of twelve trails -
You're now a member of "The Hiking Spree" -
A new polished shield yearly entails.

Some trails are difficult, others easy
Steep hills at O'Neil's woods can make one queasy.
Rock Creek Trail at Furnace Run is simple and level,
At Firestone's Red Wing Trail, birds and ducks revel.

Oxbow and Chuckery Trails at Cascade Valley
Along the Cuyahoga River, interesting sites to talley,
A three-hundred year old Burr Oak 'Indian Signal Tree'
Predates settlers who passed by before you and me.

Beavers are attracted by a dam on Heron pond
At Indian Spring Trail in Munroe Falls.
Blueberries and ferns seen while walking along,
In summer, the lake attracts picnickers and swimmers all.

Parcours Trail at both Sand Run and Goodyear Heights
Has exercise stations adults and children enjoy,
Beech-maple forests dim the light -
Hansel and Gretel feeling, girls and boys.

Chippewa Trail at Silver Creek
Features a Red Oak twenty-one feet around,
Offers many other interesting sights,
Gentle grassy slopes that abound.

THE HIKING SPREE (Con't)

Towpath Trail at Deep Lock Quarry
Provided rocks for Akron's courthouse,
Very steep up to the quarry face -
Definitely a picture taking place.

Sand Run's Mingo Trail is one of the longest
Explored mostly by the hardy and strongest,
Hampton Hills has steps to climb
Small bridges to cross, take your time.

The Gorge Trail passes Mary Campbell's Cave,
Twelve year old captured by Delaware Indian braves,
They lived on the Western Reserve temporarily,
Five years later, they set her free.

Glen's Trail passes Ohio Edison's Power Plant
Three mile long Highbridge Trail has steps to gallivant,
Both trails follow the Cuyahoga River that divides
Akron and Cuyahoga Falls, on opposite sides.

Hiking's for summer, winter, autumn, and spring,
However, harvest time will bring
Glorious nature at its peak,
Colorful leaves and wildflowers to seek.

Hope to see you there next year -
Look for us tramping the Hiking Spree,
My husband, family and friends so dear,
September 1 to November 30 jamboree.

ACME GROCERY STORES

It was in downtown Akron in eighteen ninety-one
Where Albrecht's one room store had just begun -
Fred W. and his extended family
Sold groceries on Buchtel Avenue and Center Street
Operating at a loss for eleven years
Because of credit and customers in arrears -
He changed the policy and name
To cash-only Acme chain.
From small neighborhood stores
To regional supermarkets galore,
The move forcing many out of business,
But Acme survived its stronghold,
Competition of other markets acquiesced.
It's lion's share stressed in the last decade,
Closing of Click, Y-Mart, Acme Express made.
Now Stow and Tallmadge remodeling project,
Fresh market format, downsizing addressed,
Adopting latest industry trend
To better serve customers needs,
Cafes, child care centers to render
Entertainment, socializing, satisfaction guaranteed.
One hundred eight years of quality service, the best,
Alliances and franchises their newest quest
For lovely crisp produce, and choicest cut meat,
Cleanliness and friendliness, Acme can't be beat.

THE GOODYEAR BLIMP

It glides through the air like a big balloon
Seen at dawn, twilight, or afternoon,
The Goodyear Blimp, the Spirit of Akron,
One of our country's exemplary paragons.

Huge, lighter-than-air airship
Filled with lighter-than-air gas
Cigar- shaped dirigible on advertising trips
Photographing our cities with appropriate class.

Flying high over stadiums, football games,
Lighting up the starless sky,
Cruising low, hovering over Halls of Fame,
Astonishing young or old passersby.

This envelope of synthetic fabric
Roving over land and sea,
Surveying, sightseeing, patrolling,
Pride of the land of the free.

I hope someday to have a chance
To ride in this manned aircraft
And soar through the atmosphere
Like the wind without a draft.

CUYAHOGA FALLS, OHIO
MY FAVORITE CITY

I've been to London
Toured the streets of Paris,
Of all the world's select cities,
Cuyahoga Falls is the fairest.

I've lived in Pittsburgh,
Other surrounding communities
No other area compares
To Cuyahoga Falls' many opportunities.

I've vacationed in Miami, Florida,
Los Angeles, Dallas, New Orleans,
Our metropolis has more of a
Perfect seasonal climate, harmonious scenes.

Good schools and churches, beautiful parks,
Water Works, the Nat, the river front
concerts after dark,
Shops and festivals on the malls, the font.

Clean streets, summer or winter,
Timely removal of snow,
Taylor-Memorial Library a winner,
Best locality in the nation I know.

A wholesome, peaceful place in the land
Where families and civic pride go hand in hand
A little bit of heaven is our home town
North, South, East, West, up or down.

THE CUYAHOGA WATERFALL

The river flows downstream into a roaring waterfall
A photographer's prolific dream
Rushing, gushing around breakers, mesmerizing onlookers -
Jetstream sound drowning out everything
While icicle shaped droplets dance like projectile bayonets,
The platform filled with children standing in awe
Leaning on the symmetrical wooden rail, skin dark or pale
While the sun alters the complexions
Of the living, breathing confection,
A plummeting saffron hue liquid
Till the luminous day-star disappears
Under ominous cumulus clouds,
Seniors searching rugged rocks
Where once their names were carved
Remembering days of yore and generations before
When Indians in their crude canoes
Paddled down this same river
Taking shelter in Mary Campbell's cave,
The captured young girl who was so brave.
Teens dressed in timely frocks hand in hand are locked
While their hearts thunder faster than the charging waters
that won't be led asunder.
Lovers affection leaping like the fountain of youth
keeping time with the spouting basin.
Tourists descending the steps, joining the rest on the terrace,
Some reclining on benches -
Viewing the magnificent sight quenches
Desires for peaceful scenes.
Dark of night intervenes, the waterfall still convenes.
Reluctantly ascending the stairs, relieved of worldly cares -
A day etched in memory
Of summertime and ecstasy.

THEN AND NOW

Legend has it that high schools are somewhat the same,
A history of teachers, teens, curriculum remain
In graduates hearts forever endowed,
Fruitful memories of Cuyahoga Falls High School
And friendships
Then and now.

Potpourri of students starting their freshman year,
Some nonchalant, some full of fear
Not knowing what the future foretells
What clique to join, which subjects will jell,
It's all in learning how
Then and now.

Sophomores hop to a different tune,
But get in sync with the dance very soon,
From college prep to manual toil,
Jitterbugging or rock and roll
The giggles, the frown on the brow
Then and now.

Serious juniors choose their life's work
Some serious couples, some lovers berserk,
The halls could tell of its many tales
Of selection, rejection, woe and wails,
Teachers, coaches, counselors prevail
Then and now.

THEN AND NOW (con't)

English, Latin, biology, algebra, art, sports,
Choir, band, majorettes, cheerleaders, clubs
Proms, Homecoming King and Queen of sorts
The M & M's trophy winning ways
Make for constructive, educational, fun days
Then and now.

A senior studies very hard,
Commencement looms on every card,
Future leaders of the community
Exploring every advancement opportunity
Always trying to do their best
Then and now.

The Alma Mater sung sincerely,
Tears for memories held so dearly
Overcoming problems and adversity
Recognizing differences and diversity
Soaring to loftier heights
Then and now.

Cuyahoga Falls High School

BACK TO THE GORGE

The shrill cawing of the lowly crow,
The faint rustle of the changing leaves,
The thundering waterfall below
The familiar trail that winds and weaves.
Hiking through the Gorge
As summer turns to fall
Brings back fond memories
Of other autumns' call.
Exploring dank and murky caves,
Climbing moss-covered rugged rocks
With hearts so young and brave
We took our yearly nature walks
Tip-toeing across intimidating pipes,
Foraging narrow passages,
Fearlessly fording challenging breakers,
Invincible, carefree teenagers.
Now the same trail lures us once again
With new wooden bridges to cross -
We balance ourselves with a hiking stick,
The pleasures of outdoor life never lost.

BOULEVARD OF DREAMS

Two sided byway
Island of green in between
Flowers in brilliant array,
Daffodils and tulips in season
Decorated for every holiday.
Yearly parade on Memorial Day
Veterans carrying Old Glory
Commencing patriotic story.
Flags, red, white and blue
Fourth of July display
Fluttering in the sweltering heat
Pulsing the Flower City's beat.
Frightful displays enhance Halloween,
Ghostly creatures, imaginary scenes.
All year long the carousel horses prance -
Heads turn to enjoy Broad Boulevard's dance.
Lighting the Christmas tree
Choirs singing joyfully,
Children's eyes sparkling
Like the blinking lights and decorations,
Broad Boulevard's holiday creations.
Winter's encroaching icicle fingers
Paint trees, frosted wonderland harbinger
Of refreshing spring
A celebration of life
And the joy of living.

19

THE LAST HOUSE IN THE FALLS

North to south, east to west,
The last house in the Falls was the best
Because we lived there.
Uptown, downtown, all around town,
Even when walls came tumbling down
Our spirit lived there.
Scrubbing, cleaning, washed with tears,
We lived our early formative years,
Building up, tearing apart,
Nails striking deep within our hearts,
Working, smiling, caring -
Feats that resembled daring,
Father that strayed, mother that stayed,
Walking floors, closing, opening doors,
New additions of wood and cement,
Added structures to build and lament
But a fortress in the storms,
The last house in the Falls to store
Fond memories of love, togetherness, more
Because we LIVED there.

MAKING WAVES AT THE NAT

' Twas seven years ago, the doctor said,
"Stop the high impact land exercises,
Do water aerobics instead
Or you'll have surgery on your knee."
"No way," thought I, "no knife for me"
I'll take the warm water any day
Even with cold dressing rooms (I'll say!)
Or warm dressing rooms and cold water -
Any which way.

At the Cuyahoga Falls Natatorium
I've been instructed by many,
Wilma, Ginny, Patty, Connie, Mandy, and Tammy,
Misty, Sue, Peg, Susan, and Barb -
Have I forgotten any?
I've liked them all and all their styles
Their knowledge, their workouts
And their smiles.

I've met many people who became good friends,
The joy of new acquaintances never ends.
The luncheons, the parties, the picnics, the food
The games, the jokes, the compatible moods,
Vince, Julie, the rest
Who graciously service the front desk
All make life better and hopefully longer,
Healthier, happier, wealthier, stronger.

21

THE CLOCK THAT TIME FORGOT

It haunts the walls of the Front Street Mall,
Its intricate mechanism revealed to all,
Not keeping time, baffling City Hall
And clock makers, electricians, and engineers -
Masquerading as a precision timekeeper,
But never stalling the Grim Reaper -
The brand new clock on the Mall.
Saving time or swallowing it up like an immense ocean -
The most valuable thing a human can spend,
Making time count until the end
Instead of counting time.
The clock that forgot time or time forgot,
Making daily changes, like it or not,
Passing us all, fading away,
Astonished by how many minutes we catch in a day,
For old Father Time kills us all,
Rich, poor, great and small,
The invention of the clock
Will not save us by killing time.
Time well used brings fortune, luck and name,
Gnawing away everything else
But powerless against truth
Which is always the same.
Let the measure of time be not mechanical
But spiritual
With deep life and noble moments;
Let the clock be a conversation piece -
As time goes by, this, too, shall cease -
It's just a matter of time.

OH, DEER

Three young deer scampering up the hill
Startled by voices in the morning chill,
Hikers walking along the trail
Covered by damp brown leaves that fell
During the twilight mist, the gentle rain
Of Indian summer once again.

One small deer running up Seventh Street
Panicked by traffic it might meet
Ducking through and around back yards
To find a way home to the park
From whence it came -
No one expected to see game

People pointing fingers, shouting "SEE THE DEER"
Unusual sight on the concrete paving -
The talk of the neighborhood for a day -
Hope "BAMBI" found its way
Back home to family,
That's the only safe place for a deer to be.

For a while
Until hunting season
When sportsmen seem to find a reason
To stalk and slaughter innocent deer -
'Tis said it benefits nature and provides venison -
I just say "Poor little dears."

SHADOWS OF THE CROSS

Three shadows cast upon the wall
By the cross of Jesus dangling on a rope -
Shadows prompting past recall
Of St. Joseph's Church, charity, faith and hope.

The shadow of struggle in my youth
For sustenance of body and soul,
Searching always for the truth,
Knowledge, wisdom and self-control.

The ceiling elaborately painted with Angels
Was beautiful and awesome to behold -
Jesus, His Mother Mary, and Joseph,
His birth, His life and love retold..

A visit later with my young daughter,
A curious and beautiful child
Who looked up and asked, "Mother,
Are we in heaven?" She was beguiled.

The art work has since been replaced
By wooden beams and paint off-white,
The cross hangs now in the center,
Three shadows cast by window light.

The second shadow is the present,
Carrying His cross of pain each day
Intermingled with the joy of living,
Joining our Saviour along the way.

The third shadow is the future
Which could be long or brief -
Will we join Him in heaven
Just as He promised the thief?

The Church's interior decor has changed
But the exterior remains the same,
All lives to be enriched and rearranged -
Those shadows to follow again.

OAKWOOD CEMETERY

Everyone loves a parade
Cheering while marching bands play,
Batons hurled high in the air
On Memorial Day in our city so fair.

Veterans proudly carry their banners,
Crowds stand in respect, proper manners
As flags, blowing in the breeze, are held high,
On Fourth Street as they walk by.

Turning the corner to Oakwood Cemetery
Where eulogies are given for service to country,
Graves marked by plain white crosses,
Tears shed for all our losses.

Flowers planted by somber headstones
In remembrance of sacrifice -
To save our country's freedom
These young soldiers have given their life.

The parade of life goes by
Like cymbols echoing in the distance
Too soon we live and then we die -
No one but God can control the dance.

CRYSTAL FAREWELL

The delicate crystal palace on both sides of the road,
Elegant snow taking shape on each tree's limbs like a cape
Lined along Riverside Drive, across the Gorge to Front Street
An ornate wonderland of ice magic, frosted shaped twigs unfold
Enchantment out of this world,
Fingers dipping into a frozen bowl
or pointing upwards into the mist,
Ghosts dancing eerily in the breeze,
The month of March so fickle,
A coated vessel, a cup of freeze
Fashioned by the season's ripple -
Winter's lingering farewell.

WINDOW WATCHING

It was Thanksgiving day,
We gratefully ate the feast, put the dishes away,
Bundled the children in winter coats -
Frigid wintry day, snowflakes softly afloat.
Jumped in the car without any care
Anticipation of Christmas joy in the air,
Drove the whole family downtown to see
Polsky's and O'Neils windows, the Christmas tree -
Animated animals decorating outstretched branches
Old fashioned dolls revolving, doing their dances,
Mrs. Claus baking cookies and candy,
Santa's sleigh piled high with toys just dandy.
From corner to corner, eyes eager to see
This lively portrayal of their fantasy.
Tiny elves building toys with hammer and nails,
Jack and Jill tumbling losing their pail,
Angels in white garments with golden wings
Over the lowly manger, the King of Kings,
Oh, how we miss each fascinating windowpane -
Still, memories of tradition and kinship forever remain.

FRIVOLOUS SATIN

Glimmering, shimmering, elegant satin
Yearning for it in Cleveland, Canton and Akron,
Rag-a-muffin, prim and proper, or in-between,
Altering the scenario from what has been.
Destitute who accept cotton or polyester,
Haughty who neglect and let fester
Attitudes of hurt and frustration.
Idealists who skim above the surface
To rebuild, renew, and refurbish
Society crying for attention -
Causes too numerous to mention;
Multitudes agonizing in tatters
Relinquishing values that matter.
Caucasion, African-American, Asian or Latin,
Searching for elusive, but attainable, satin.
Be wary about what you're longing for
Lest with fulfillment you slide to the floor -
Slippery, frivolous, impractical satin.

TREASURE BY THE SHORE

Cleveland was never a mistake by the lake

Although other cities may have called it that -

From industry, ethnic, racial diversity

To the Jake,

To the Rock-N-Roll Hall of Fame

Where The Beatles, Elvis, & Kiss are famous names,

To the Great Lakes Science Center

With its weather forecaster and rocket flight simulator,

Its bubble machine, shadow and tornado maker,

A hot air balloon that rises to the top,

To Playhouse Square, Euclid Avenue, Tower City to shop,

To the Flats, Gund Arena, the Cavs,

The return of the Browns football team,

Cleveland, Ohio is Lake Erie's spectacular scene.

CANTON'S PRO FOOTBALL HALL OF FAME
1999

Many renowned names are enshrined
In Canton's Pro Football Hall of Fame,
Busts of famous football players lined
From Jim Thorpe to Ozzie Newsome,
Jim Brown and Marion Motley,
The latter area threesome.
Each year their prowess is acclaimed
And new appointees are proudly named.
A correlated parade - a football game played -
New Cleveland Browns and Dallas Cowboys in '99,
Bernie Kosar, Bob Golic, other celebrities combine,
Tailgate parties, barking Dawgs,
Painted faces, arms, canine togs
Shouting, chanting GO BROWNS -
BEAT THE COWBOYS -
Victory was theirs - 20 to 17,
Browns intensity as always pristine,
Good start for the long awaited season,
Spectators from Pennsylvania,
Indiana, Illinois, Michigan,
Hotels filled to capacity,
Yearly August tenacity.

BARBERTON'S LAKE ANNA

Children can be seen feeding the ducks,
Seniors sitting on benches or walking,
Fishermen trying to catch their luck,
Geese gatherings continue their stalking.

This exquisite body of water catches the eye
Reflections of leaves on trees as one strolls by,
Festivals held here, water and craft shows,
Bands and orchestras play music in the gazebo.

Daffodil and tulip beds in the spring,
Festival of mums autumn will bring,
White, mauve, maize, rust, flame patterned hues,
Breathtaking, exhilarating, unbelievable views.

Beauty pageants and parades on historical days,
Military Honor Roll for veterans who served in wars,
Cannon exhibited commemorating wartime days,
Bells tolling from St. Augustine's church not far.

If you are looking for somewhere to go
On any pleasant day, any season
Lake Anna is the place you should know
That delights any time, for any reason.

RAVENNA'S BALLOON A-FAIR

An awesome sight on three consecutive nights -
A children's parade on Main Street,
Hot-air balloons launched from Sunbeau Valley Farm site,
Crafts, music, and funnel cakes to eat.
From its earliest industry 'toy manufacturing' days
Ravenna's celebration has grown in numerous ways -
From a pumpkin festival and antique show
To over two hundred exhibitors.
High clouds, and light northwesterly winds make
Perfect weather to go
Up, up and away in the beautiful balloons that soar
Into the serene silence of the sky
Broken only by occasional propane heaters' roar
As the procession of pilots and passengers float by,
A colorful display of dazzling designs
That take your breath away!

HISTORIC TALLMADGE CIRCLE

If you don't do circles
You may want to rethink your route
And travel all the back roads
To avoid going in and out
The maze of entrances to
The Tallmadge circle.

If you do do circles
Tallmadge Circle's the best way to go
To Akron, Hudson, Cuyahoga Falls,
Brimfield, Ellet, Mogadore and Stow.
If you get mixed up and go around twice
The historic Congregational church makes it seem nice
On Tallmadge Circle.

If you stop off at the circle
To shop or browse at Bumpas Emporium,
You may later want to jaunt
Over for lunch at a restaurant
On Tallmadge Circle.

If you happen to live in Tallmadge,
You had better like circles all ways,
For the traffic there can engage you
In going around in circles all day.
On Tallmadge Circle.

Tallmadge, even with the circle
Is a charming community in which to live.
Residents take their sports seriously
And have much civic pride to give
All around Tallmadge Circle.

LAND AND SEA FUN

Let's take a trip to Sea World
One of only three in the United States,
People drive from nearby and all over
To Aurora where water creature fun awaits.

Starting early in the morning
Meandering from show to show,
Dolphins, penguins, sea lions, Shamu
Splashing spectators in seats below.

Children exploring the Pirates Cove
Climbing up Happy Harbor nets,
Dinosaurs spouting water in Carnivore park
Like syncopated jets.

Boats, water skiers, acrobats,
Stingrays flat in their habitat,
Aquariums, domestic and exotic fish.
Swim through the water, splish, splash, splish.

Let's take a trip to Geauga Lake
Amusement park across the way,
Rides and games, plunging in the Wave
All on a warm summer's day.

Indoor, outdoor musicals, dancing and singing
Midway games, people mingling
Roller coasters and carousels
Ice cream cones, apples, candied or caramel.

What better place to be
Than with our friends on land or sea
And what a lovely vacation
Seaworld and Geauga Lake celebrations.

33

HELPING HANDS

If you hear the cry of the poor, do you care?
Do you have empathy for the homeless whatever the cause?
Do you open your heart to the look of despair,
Or do you only look to see flaws?
Do you see the sad eyes of the children
Caught up in circumstances beyond their control?
They need to be comforted, they need to be consoled
With love, shelter, clothing, and food
To end their suffering, their lives renewed.
Red Cross volunteers the world over rescue all nations
From natural disasters,
earthquakes, tornadoes, hurricanes, floods,
But in our little corner of the world
The Haven of Rest offers assistance for the oppressed
And rehabilitation programs for the depressed.
Good Neighbors provide clothing and food baskets at holidays,
The shelter for battered women helps save them
From indignities and violence
No one should endure any day.
Open M (and some churches) serve hot lunches,
Offer tutoring and mentoring, too,
Moving families out of poverty,
Stimulating hope, faith and energy.
All helping hands that kindly bestow
The blessings we take for granted
Thank God we have people who show
Compassion and love for the unfortunate
Human beings they don't even know.

MARY ANN JAMESON

Mary Ann Jameson was born in Akron, Ohio, on October 4, 1942. Her parents were James R. and Florence Jameson. She has three brothers, her best friends.

Mary Ann attended St. Martha School and Central High School.

She has loved poetry her entire life. Her deep love of God has lead her to write inspirational poetry over the years to give hope to the hopeless, to encourage others not to give up, and to know that with God, all things are possible.

Her work has appeared in many publications including:
THE CHRISTIAN WAY
THE POET'S VOICE
LINES N' RHYMES
BRYON POETRY WORKS
SALESIAN MISSIONS

Mary Ann has also been published in several poetry Anthologies, and has won several awards, including the "Blue Ribbon Award" from the Southern Poetry Association.

ST. BERNARD'S CATHOLIC CHURCh
(on the National Register of Historic Places)

In the heart of downtown Akron,
Shines a precious jewel.
It's twin spires touch the heavens -
Of lovely azure blue.

A dream of early settlers-
In eighteen sixty one,
Forty-six true believers,
Built their house of God.

It's beginnings, very humble-
As their small brick structure stood.
Their congregation growing,
But, they did what they could.

Then, their dream got bigger.
They saw it, crystal clear
A "Cathedral" was their vision
But, this dream would take years.

Years of prayer and planning.
Funds were raised and saved.
At last, their plan in motion.
The way was clearly paved.

From our local quarry,
The stonework it did come.
The stained-glass, all from Germany.
Exquisite work, well done.

The altars came from Italy.
Pure marble, grand and fair.
Their "dream"; this great cathedral
At last, it all was here.

God's house at last completed
In nineteen zero five.
A concert then was given
And its doors, now open wide.

36

HOWER HOUSE
(National Historic Landmark)
(Akron, Ohio)

In my own fair city,
stands a house; unique and rare.
Completed in eighteen seventy-one.
It's style, beyond compare.

Designed by John Henry Hower,
and Architect, Jacob Snyder.
In Second Empire Italianate style -
mansard roof and soaring tower.

This twenty-eight room mansion,
is filled with treasures galore.
It's furnishings quite exquisite
Gathered from'round the world.

For three generations they lived there.
Then in nineteen seventy
They deeded it over, this generous gift,
to our fine University.

The house is now open for touring.
Visitors will get to see
All the beauty and all splendor,
This gift from the Hower family.

37

WHERE QUAKER OATS BEGAN

Once in my fair city
A bustling factory stood.
Where Quaker Oats, a grain mill
With lofty silos loomed.

I will always remember,
When I went into town,
The scent of fresh milled oats
Was wafting all around.

But just as life has changes,
The factory moved away.
It stood as silent witness,
To things of yesterday.

Today, its transformation
Is something to behold.
A hotel/shopping complex,
Its design is brave and bold..

The silos, new hotel rooms
Where oat grain once was stored.
These ultramodern guest rooms
Are really much adored.

The factory, now a complex,
Of fine shops, grand and fair,
The DEPOT, that's for dining,
With model railroads there.

It's still hard to imagine.
At times, I stop and stare.
To think that mill and factory,
Is now grand, QUAKER SQUARE.

THE SOAP BOX DERBY

In Akron every summer,
A great event is held.
A quite grand competition,
Where cars race down a hill.

The cars, homemade by children,
"Soap Boxes" they are called,
Are raced by local chanpions
From here and 'round the world.

The contest stresses fairness,
Good sportsmanship, that's true.
The winner gets a trophy,
And a check for money too!

The day is always festive,
And a grand parade is held,
With celebrities, the "Oil Can" race,
In oversized cars, as well.

The day full of excitement,
A family time for sure,
I pray this wonderful event,
That it always will endure.

IT'S MORE THAN JUST A TRAIN RIDE
(The Cuyahoga Valley Scenic Railroad)

It rings across the valley,
And it echoes off the hills.
As it travels back through history,
This ride is full of thrills.

As it slowly travels,
Wonders then unfold.
The animals in the valley,
Make their presence known.

The trees are full of song birds,
The woods are full of deer.
The waterfowl are drifting,
On water, cool and clear.

The beavers, they are busy,
Building a new dam.
Also, herons and coyotes -
Hawks and rabbits in the land.

Historic sites are on the route
As it travels through the valley
There's Inventure Place, Quaker Square
And also, Deep Lock Quarry.

There's Stan Hywet Hall and Gardens,
Hale Farm and Village, too.
A Peninsula adventure,
Is waiting just for you.

The Canal Visitor Center,
Is a wonderful museum.
Learn about canal days,
With a canal lock demonstration.

With Indian Mound, and ski resorts.
A wonder every season.
A great adventure can be yours,
And now you know the reason!

RAY KLUG

Ray Klug, born August 16, 1929, Akron, Ohio, attended
St. Bernard's School, and Central High School.

He entered the Armed Services in 1951, took light and heavy
infantry weapons course at Ft. Benning, Georgia, and graduated.
This course teaches outstanding non-commissioned officers
of the Army methods of instruction, leadership and various
sundry techniques of modern infantry warfare.

Ray has written stories for various magazines and newspapers.
He has also appeared on television.   Stories regarding him have
been written in several newspapers, including the Beacon Journal.

He wrote five best selling books, two of them encyclopedias,
under the title ANTIQUE ADVERTISING.

His first poem was written in 1995. He also writes Liners, and
has begun to write Short Stories. His memories of the old Akron
still remain.

He now resides in Wadsworth, Ohio.

THE POETS

I know feelings of those that write poetry.
For this gift, a friend gave to me.
Disruptive things can't be around
If a poem is to be found.

The mind will wander in every way
Looking for the right words to say.
We relate many things we went through;
Many poems and parts are so true.

There are times that will bring the tears
As our thoughts go through so many years.
Make believe, is such a small part
What's been lived and seen, is in our heart.

So many poems with the truth told
Gives the readers our thoughts to hold.
It gets lonely trying to write a poem
For the most part, we're all alone.

Writing poems does take our stress away
For sorrow that may have been caused yesterday.
Many of our thoughts may seem profound,
But we write what our hearts have found.

There are poems written with negative thoughts;
On the other side, what beauty has brought.
Writing poems surely works on the mind
When done, pride is what we find.

It's another world brought to you
From a poets point of view.
You may read of our dreams
Or of the things that were seen.

We're the poets who with you, we share
The sorrow and beauty that's found everywhere.
Our feelings, you can all see
From us who write the poetry.

MY TOWN

I was born and raised in Akron town...
Many things I remember are no longer around
My neighborhood being mostly Italian and German;
The center, being at Cross St. and Sherman.

Looking beyond, Buchtel Field could be found
For dancing, East Market Gardens was around.
On weekends, Summit Beach Park with the Midway,
And all the theaters, my hero's would play.

Then Lake Anna, such a beautiful park,
Where I sat many times after dark.
We had canoes we'd always take,
As we headed for the Portage Lakes.

There were steam engines that chugged on through,
With their lonely whistles out of view.
Now and then, a dirigible in the sky...
These always seemed to catch the eye.

Family reunions back then was a big thing;
Together, all the relatives, they would bring.
Front porches that faced the street,
Where for hours, neighbors and friends would greet.

Clubs, buildings and homes have gone with time
Leaving so many memories in my mind.
I ask, can there ever be another day
Like those that went on their way?

REMEMBERING

I walked the streets that are in my mind...
Streets that come from another time.
At main and Howard, The Flat Iron Building, I see,
Here, the smell of Quaker Oats is brought to me.

On Grant St., Burkhardt's Brewery with the smell of beer,
With the twelve o'clock whistle, I can still hear.
Here too, the City Bakery whose pastries we shared,
As the smell of sweetness filled the air.

At Grant and South Street, another name to be found,
For this area, at one time, was called "goose town."
Across Sherman Street, I could never forget,
'Wolf Ledges' with tales from old timers I met.

The Exchange Street bridge, many times made my day,
As I watched the trains come and go on their way.
I'll never forget what they left behind,
For black soot on my clothes, I would find.

The one sight that will always be with me,
Are St. Bernard's steeples that remain to see.
They seem to touch every cloud that goes by,
With such grace brought to the eye.

There are things that remain the same,
And most streets still have their name.
There are many corners yet to be turned,
And things of the past still to be learned.

As we age, with our memories, we can find
A little history that comes to our mind.
These thoughts, we pass on with care
So those in the future can share.

FRANKIE SPETICH

A lifetime of music brought with cheer;
Music we hold in our hearts so dear,
Whenever needed, you were always there,
Playing your music for all to share.

I talked with you many times,
You related music on your mind.
Traveling never seemed to be a big thing;
Happiness with your music, you would bring.

Yes, there were so many years and places,
As you played, you could see happy faces.
Your recordings, and what you wrote,
You played beautifully, right to the note.

A radio program brought you to the air
With you, another way for us to share,
Teaching Button Box came your way,
With happy students who wanted to play.

Through life, it wasn't easy many times,
But you always had a determined mind.
Age for many of us, takes its toll,
But for you, it was just go and go.

I always thought you deserve so much more
For a lifetime and places playing your score.
Yes, you were made "man of the year".
Such a deserving thing for some cheer.

You lifted many hearts with the sound
Wherever your music could be found.
Your music will always go on and on
Long after you and I are gone.

Frankie Spetich, don't ever let your music end,
And thank you for being a special friend.
Some day, with Angels you will play,
And I'll be there that glorious day.

THE WEEPING ICON
1997

I had to see, and the tears were there.
Immediately I knelt and said a prayer.
A miracle many never get to see,
And to store such a beautiful memory.

The curious and skeptics were there;
The smell of roses filled the air.
Many rosaries people did hold;
Some turning from silver to gold.

"Why Here? Many would say,
In a little church our of the way."
Angry neighbors wanted to destroy it all;
Threats and dirty language they would call.

This scared many who came to pray;
One man came forth and had this to say,
"I'm little and old, you can see,
But your games will end with me."

Summoned to the prosecutors office for his deed,
The jail time he sure didn't need.
When it was over, yes, he had won;
The beginning of new days for everyone.

I went back and in the burning candles glow,
I knelt and said, "Blessed Virgin, I love you so."
This poem is true as many know.
I'm the old man in that candles glow.

VALUES

Have our lives become as such
As values no longer mean so much?
Has respect been thrown to the wayside,
And compassion we now hide?

Have we become so full of greed
That it's ourselves that only need?
Is it that we've become torn apart
Leaving many with such a cold heart?

Has it come to words that we hear . . .
Are of profanity brought to our ears?
Can it be, many have never been taught;
Now to others, this is what they brought?

Is there no love ever to be shown?
Was it disrespect taught in their home?
Yes, these are the weeds
That come from the bad seeds.

These are things not meant to share,
That come with the dirty air.
For those, there's always hope to be found;
For so many lives have been turned aorund.

You have to be willing to yield,
And throw away your shield.
All it takes is a little prayer...
You'll find love that you can share.

Forgiving is a word that's so kind,
It'll be given for peace of your mind.
With this, you'll be set free,
And the other side of life you'll see.

MY WORLD

Where's the world I used to know,
With its beauty that seems to go?

There were so many beautiful spots,
That are now asphalt parking lots.

All the buildings that have come to hide
What once was a beautiful countryside.

Birds and animals have been pushed away
By those who call this "progress" today.

So many trees have been cut down
For another business to be found.

Where's all the two lane roads
That can no longer carry traffic loads?

The peace and serenity I once did see,
Is now pollution and noise brought to me.

Was this meant to carry in my mind
The wildflowers and streams I no longer find?

What of dirt found in the country air,
Brought by those who didn't seem to care?

Is it my world has begun to fade
Because of things man has made?

How far will I have to go
To find the world I used to know?

MEITA MARSHALL

Meita Marshall was born in Chicago, Ill, on Jan. 16, 1917, of Russian-Jewish ancestry, her parents having emigrated to the United States in 1915. At the death of her father in 1921, her widowed mother placed Meita and her younger brother in an oprhan home as 'day children,' and worked in a sweatshop as a factory worker - sewing being the only trade she had practiced in the 'old country' since age ten.

When Meita graduated from high school at the height of the Depression, she worked at whatever jobs were available, from dime-store clerk to office clerk. In 1941, mother and daughter travelled to Los Angeles, California, where they decided to remain. Meita did secretarial work. In 1943, she joined the Army Air Force as a WAC, and spent the rest of the war at Wright-Patterson Air Base in Ohio. In 1947, she married John W. Marshall, and they soon migrated to his family farm in Columbiana County, five miles from Salem, Ohio, where they lived for over twenty-eight years. The couple had five children (three girls and two boys.)

John died in 1975, and Meita became a student at Kent State University, where she lived in student housing. She obtained two degrees, one in History and English, and one in Library Science. As she was almost of retirement age, she couldn't find a job in that field, so she moved to Akron, where at age eighty-two, she is now residing.

She enjoys reading, writing, folk songs, talking to all kinds of people, politics and just loving life.

WORDS

I love to talk
And if I couldn't
How sad Life
Would be!

I love the feel of words
Hitting the tissues
Of my mouth
Against my tongue
And teeth;
Words so alive
So meaningful
And so rich
With the experience
Of the human race!

Every work was
Once a feat
Of some proud culture
Of some group
Of people
Who before my time
Strode across
Our earth.
Every work
Presents a story
Of the past or present;
Every work pictures
A dream for the future.

I do not like to
Talk just to myself
I must talk
To other people
And that is
The most amazing
Thing about words.

It is the ideas
That make
Words so wonderful!
Ideas that give us
Hope and pleasure
Joy and sadness;
Ideas that create
Discord and dissension
And yet in the end
Only become
Monuments and measures
Of our thoughts
And deeds
Across the span
Of the centuries.

THE PUBLIC LIBRARY

A city in a city -
Wherever I may be,
I always feel contented
In a Public Library.

All the world's great knowledge
Is spread in front of me
Everytime I enter
A Public Library.

However I am thinking
Or what my mood may be,
I see it down in printing
At the Public Library.

The noblest thoughts of people -
Their words to set us free;
They stand on shelves like guardians
At the Public Library.

Science of the ages,
Math, technology -
In detail are assembled
At the Public Library.

Literature and music,
Art and poetry -
A feast to thrill my senses
At the Public Library.

Though wealth is not my portion,
It never meant much to me,
For I found greater treasure
At the Public Library.

Oh, you unwritten heroes
Who made libraries free,
How could I have existed
With no Public Library?

RATS IN THE GHETTO

Rats in the Ghetto
Want something to eat;
Biting and chewing
At my baby's feet.
Rats in the Ghetto
Beady-eyed, strong,
Stay right in my home
As though they belong.
Rats in the Ghetto
Gnawing away
In the walls and the floors
By night and by day.
The Ghetto is rotten,
The beams crack and fall;
Rats in the Ghetto
Dig graves for us all.

Rats in the Ghetto -
Some two-legged ones,
Disgracing our daughters
Destroying our sons -
Rats in the Ghetto sleek-skinned and fat,
They may look like humans
But they're just plain "rat."
Rats in the Ghetto put me in a cage,
Charge me high prices,
Won't pay me a wage;
Keep digging away
At my manhood and pride
'Till like the Ghetto,
I'm rotting inside.

RATS IN THE GHETTO
(con't)

Rats in the Ghetto
Say: look how you shirk,
Living on Welfare,
Don't want to work.
Rats in the Ghetto
Say be good and pray,
While they get rich, sucking
My life-blood away.
Rats in the Ghetto
I'm watching you!
I'm sitting around here
With 'nothing to do.'
You sneak into holes,
You think I don't know
That you help the cause
Of my terror and woe.

Rats in the Ghetto,
Your day is through!
Won't help if you hide,
Cause I'm wise to you!
Rats in the Ghetto,
I'll tear you apart;
Break up the Ghetto,
Get a new start!
Rats in the Ghetto,
I'll soon make an end
Of you two-legged rats;
Then take care of your friends
The four-legged ones
Who'll run fast as they can
When the Ghetto is gone
And I act like a man!

EULOGY

Great is the man who feels Life's wrong
And turns his sorrow into song.

Who takes his fear, and pain, and dread,
And makes them his 'pillars of strength' instead.

For some men sadness always traces
A shower of teardrops on their faces.

And others, dry-eyed, quietly stare
While their hearts are crushed with dull despair.

But fortunate indeed is he
Who sings when he feels Life's tragedy.

Who seeks beyond the petty schemes
That draw up many a small man's dreams.

And if his world should crumble away,
The song in his soul will ever stay.

For he who tells his secret sorrow,
Can better build a new tomorrow.

Though Life may give me nary a thing,
Let me never forget to sing!

LAND MY LAND - (Song)

Have you ever seen my farm in Ohio,
It's large rolling fields of golden gleaming corn;
Have you ever heard the cattle gently lowing,
In beautiful Ohio, the state where I was born?

CHORUS - Land, my land, oh how I love you!
           I've worked just for you, these many, many years!
           Land, my land, I dream only of you -
           You've shared all my hopes, and dried all my tears.

Have you ever felt the early morning stillness,
Have you ever smelled the new-mown hay?
Have you ever known the glory of the harvest,
When earth's growing treasures are safely stored away?

Have you ever heard the robins in the morning?
Have you ever watched the sunset in the sky -
Have you ever breathed the fragrance of the lilacs,
Or slept while wind and rain are humming nature's lullaby?

I'M JUST A HOUSEWIFE
Can be sung to Rock-a-bye Baby -

I'm just a housewife, doing my chores
Cooking and cleaning, sweeping the floors,
Just a dull housewife, tired as can be,
Spending a lifetime in bored drudgery.

I'm just a housewife, mother to all;
When my folks need me, I'm at their call
Just a worn housewife, so sad to see -
Slave to the people who say they love me.

I'm just a housewife, I know some day
My kids will grow up and move away.
Just an old housewife they can't afford
Sent to a rest home to reap her reward.

CATHERINE PLATT

Catherine Platt was born in New Philadelphia, Ohio,
in 1913,
daughter of C. Edson and Frances Catherine Creal.
She had two brothers and one sister.

She attended elementary school and high school there and
is a graduate of Muskingham College,
majoring in education.

For thirty-two years, she taught all grades,
but mostly second grade.

She married Peter Platt in 1940. They both loved to
dance and travel.

Catherine now lives at Rockynol Presbyterian Home,
Akron, Ohio

OHIO IN SPRING

These lovelies I see as I sit in my swing,
Delighting in beauty which nature does bring
For us to enjoy in Ohio each spring.

The graceful white dogwood, when seen at a glance,
Seems so dainty and fairy-like, as each spreading branch
Shows the charm of a ballerina in dance.

The maple tree in its new dress of green,
Proudly is wearing it like a queen,
And on its branch a blue jay is seen.

The leafy spirea over-flowing with grace,
Droops tiny sprigs with cluster-like lace,
Giving white loveliness to our lawn and place.

I would like to capture the lilac's sweet bloom
And hide it secretly in my room,
To enjoy forever its exquisite perfume.

There are many words at our command.
Trying to use the best at hand,
My gratitude to expand.

For glory felt within today,
As I feast upon this grand array,
I find just heart-felt, "Thank you God," to say.

ROCKYNOL SUMMER 1989

Daily for sun we have anticipation
But we receive only precipitation.
So it seems we must look for good in the rain,
And count some blessings from it, which we gain.

The lawns and hillsides are beautifully green,
And the walks, roads, even cars are extra clean.
This summer gardeners enjoy liberation
From the tedious chore of irrigation.

Children like to watch rain bubbles in the street,
And wading in puddles, to them is a treat.
We look from our window at the trees so lush,
The rich shades of green resemble velvet plush.

We all know that the rain will cease sometime,
So meanwhile, let us make our own sunshine.

OUR NATION

When reading of immortality, greed and lack,
I feel depressed and angry and want to slap back
At leaders in high office who abuse our trust,
And accumulate millions by deceit and lust.
Then I gaze from my window and ponder at length.
From gentle clouds and majestic trees I gain strength,
And I know that God governs His great creation,
In spite of turmoil, it is still a great nation.

MY MAGIC CARPET

If I could travel anywhere,
Where would I go?
I would hop on my magic carpet
And fly to fabulous Rio.

Then I would sail to the Taj Mahal,
To see that sparkling shrine.
From there I'd swiftly take
A cruise upon the Rhine.

Next on the list would be the Alps
To view the Matterhorn great.
From there I'd zoom to Geneva
And scan that lovely lake.

Another place I would enjoy
Is the British Countryside,
And the famous pyramids,
Then on the Nile I'd ride.

The statues on Easter Island
Are worthy to behold.
No one knows how they were carved
Is the story I am told.

They, like the stones at Stonehenge,
Are such a mystery.
Oh dear, this world affords
So very much to see.

But my carpet is getting thin;
It has put so many miles in.
So I must fly back home today,
And for awhile, there I'll stay.

DREAMA POWELL

Dreama S. Powell
Falls High '66
University of Akron '77 (BFA)

Serving actively in these organizations:

Northamption Historical Society
Scottish Harp Society of America
Akron Area Poetry Society
WOW Chapter of the National Story-telling League

Serving semi-actively in these organizations:

Perkins Parlor Players
Daughters of Scotia

Life member of the Bronte Society.

EDWARD ROLAND SILL 1841-1887

From Windsor, Connecticut of old stock,
came Edward Roland Sill to our flock,
A graduate of Yale, the educational block.

He graced our town with high caliber,
Teaching, and High School arbitrator,
A transcendental elevator!

What a lucky privilege
to be under such a tutelage,
in the 19th century; a classic age.

It was a time of staid influence.
Parlors were a place of confluence;
Churches flourished in abundance.

He married his cousin, Elizabeth Newberry Sill,
after America's Civil strife was still.
and taught at the High School on the east hill.

Away they went to live in California a year.
They must have missed their home back here,
for they returned to their relatives so dear.

His poetry won him national fame,
This gentleman with a genius flame.
His legacy now is a school bearing his name.

But his fine mansion could not stay,
The Sutliff Apartments got in the way.
His whole era has vanished away.

At Oakwood Cemetery's lonely Poet's hill,
at age 46, rests Edward Roland Sill.
He is a treasure for us still.

As his gravestone dissolves too
He left words for me and for you,
That are always fresh and new.

NORTHAMPTON

Northampton's fields and township square
are now gone and being laid bare.
Mary Cereke's woods are tamed,
not much left that can be named.
The school is Woodridge now
and you hardly ever see a cow.

Sadly, the names of Harrington and Prior
are now behind a cemetery wire.
The farms were grand and spacious,
all the neighbors, friendly and gracious.
The city people may think it strange
but descendents belong to the "Grange".

Where kindly folk, the husbandry gather
at the Town Hall, a community treasure.
You may still glimpse a barn,
where milk cans clinked in the morn,
and farmers stacked them on a stand
at the Center of this township land.

Who knows what is in Northampton's future?
As the city absorbs the agriculture,
just how far can urban sprawl
destroy everything with another Mall?
How we'd like to keep,
the brooks of water and forests deep!

ROCKIN' ON THE RIVER

Universal Loud
What does it mean to you?
Does it empower, mesmerize,
obliterate the world?
Does it jar blast you into
another consciousness?
Rattling through your bones,
a vibrating nervousness.
Does it envelop you in
A safe place from the silence,
Or is it a numbness
When it stops that delights?
Do you also know of the finesse?
Those quiets of crickets and lace wings,
The delicate pulses in life.
Ultimate Beat.
The lyrics do not matter,
With all the party people's chatter;
Who is listening
(that can hear!)
Did I see a plug in an ear?!!

ELIZABETH FISHER SEUFFERT

Elizabeth Fisher Seuffert was born in Philadelphia, Pennsylvania. She spent a year at Gettysburg College, followed by defense work at Goodyear Aircraft in Akron, Ohio, during World War II. At the end of the war, Elizabeth attended The University of Akron and was graduated with a Bachelor of Arts Degree (English major, History minor). Later, she went to England and Wales for further education

As a published writer, she also enjoys music and has sung as a choir member and soloist at St. Luke's Lutheran Church, Cuyahoga Falls, and as soloist and flutist with groups throughout Northeastern Ohio. Besides home duties, she has interviewed on Warner Cable Television.

Recently Elizabeth and her husband celebrated their fiftieth wedding annidversary. Her husband Norman E. Seuffert, Jr., was a major in the Eighth Air Force and the Strategic Air Command. He is retired from The Village of Silver Lake, where he was head gardener. The Seufferts had four sons, two are living: Robert (married to Anice Hamby, four granddaughters: Rochelle, Nicole, Crystal and Melissa, two great-granddaughters: Brook-lynne and Dominique) and son Henry. An infant son and Thomas are deceased.

1944 - GOING TO LUNCH, SHOPPING
AND THE MOVIES

What fun it was to shop, when one was in one's teens
To meet a friend and play pretend
That we were mature human beings.

We'd take the bus to downtown shops
And have lunch at the Garden Grill
When we were through, we'd tip our girl
And pay our bill and shopping we'd pursue.

At Polsky's or O'Neils, we'd bee-line for the clothes
Then, we'd leaf through all the racks,
And, perhaps, turn up our nose.

Then, Nan, my friend, would come and say:
"Come see this dress, my dear, it's really you."
It would be weird or a ghastly one.
Not what I was after.
But it was meant to make me dissolve into laughter.

Then, I would go and do the same
For Nan, for by this time
We would know that this was not our day,
For finding anything sublime.

No special dress, I could afford,
That would make my "SPECIAL FRIEND"
Realize I was that "SPECIAL ONE"
Then, suddenly as quiet as two stalking cats
We'd try on hats.
It was really such great fun!

"Pst, Nan, look here." Upon my head,
Something like an old lady would buy
And she'd look back, wearing something black
Then, turn and raise her head high,
And mimic in profile, a foreign spy.

And we would laugh and try on more
And make all kinds of faces,
Until a clerk would come and ask:
"May I help you girls?"
And that would slow our paces.

Oh, listen Friend, this would put an end,
To our afternoon of shopping
For we would say: "No thanks, we're just looking".
And off we'd go to Loews or the Colonial
to a picture show.
Hours later, we'd come out
with stars sparkling in our eyes.

Then, when our crowded bus came by,
We'd find all seats taken and in the crush,
Hang from the straps so high.
And wonder when if war would end,
We'd ever see that "SPECIAL FRIEND".

MEMORIES OF CUYAHOGA FALLS COMMUNITY BAND

We were dedicated musicians playing at schools and fairs,
High rise apartment buildings, nursing homes and malls.
In summer, we played throughout parks in the Falls.
At Taylor Library, by the fountain we'd perform,
Or in the Sutliff Room if it started to storm.
Our opening concert in summer
was under the bridge below the Mall,
And we closed out our season there just before Fall.
Indian Mountain, Linden, Lions,
Oak and Kennedy Park pass in review.
Ross Park was named for Rowena,
A marine killed in World War ll.
Newberry, where the sky was our view,
With sun in our eyes, it was hard to play
At that time of day.
At Oak Park and Valley Vista, children played
On swings or waded in the pools.
And there were times we played at different schools:
Such as DeWitt, where a grandmother blew bubbles
For children in her care
The bubbles floated around and burst in the air.
Our band played by the arch below the Mall,
At Tallmadge Fair and other schools:
Lincoln, Schnee, Falls High
Then benefit baseball games and the days flew by.
Cuyahoga Valley National Recreation Area, we did
Lincoln Portrait there.
Memories of other events come to mind:
Westminster Strawberry Festival was one of a kind.
Ice cream socials at Bethany and at Church Park.
Our band played there until it was almost dark

67

Remember the Rib-Burn Off for the Lions Club on the Mall,
Or the concerts by the fountain, silver at day, golden at night,
But that isn't all.
The band played at the Dedication
of the Veterans Memorial on Broad Boulevard,
And the Silver Lake Festival with sailboats on the lake,
As a backdrop.
On a summer evening, where time seemed to stop.
Then, the days went by so very fast
Somehow summer did not seem to last.
At Christmas, we played for the tree lighting at Lions Lodge
And Santa Claus came.
He greeted the children and knew each name.
Solos, duets, ensembles, quartets,
Show tunes, classical music, folk songs, marches,
Christmas music and jazz
Different kinds of mood music, each tune has.
Corn roasts and picnics at Baker's Acres were family times.
Spouses, children, grandchildren swimming in the lake,
Covered dish dinners, Senior citizens at Lions Lodge
Served ice cream and cake.
Practice, practice at Bolich and Quirk
Sometimes it was fun, sometimes it was work.
But the day came when it was time to move on,
Leaving a strong organization
That started with just a few musicians.
It hadn't seemed long, when we first met,
But, those happy times, I'll never forget.

INVENTURE PLACE
Home of
THE NATIONAL INVENTORS HALL OF FAME

Inspired inventors, with or without formal education,

Have contributed their best to the world and our nation.

Persistence is the key word for all.

From Edison, who brought his genius to technology,

To a long list of men and women dedicated to physiology.

George Washington Carver was an agricultural chemist,

Improving the land, a form of ecology.

Inventors, who were curious, invented and patents secured,

Are now honored with showcases

And displays at Akron's Inventors Hall of Fame.

Along with others, too numerous to name.

A visit there and you will be glad that you came.

Creativity, imagination and discovery have led many to fame.

RHEA SHROYER

Born: December 15, 1913, in Akron, Ohio

Parents: Bert and Minnie Gaylord

Education: High School, Some College and Art

Personal: Divorced, One daughter (teacher),
Son-in-law (teacher), and Grandson (Attorney) -
Worked 57 years nonstop during which time
she raised her daughter.

Charter Member of National Secretaries Association

Charter Member of Ann Case Toastmistress Club -
Chosen Woman of the Year in 1975

Teaches Sunday School at Trinity United Church of Christ

Composed music and lyrics for church song -
GOD'S DISCIPLES

Have written poems to family and friends for many
years, published own group of poems 1977

DOWNTOWN AKRON, OHIO, YEARS AGO

Downtown Akron in years long past
Had so many places to go;
You could grab a snack or dine in style -
Then on to a show;
The evenings were packed with crowds
going here and there
If you didn't drive, there were buses lined up for your fare;
Garden Grille, Roxys Cafe, or Stones Grille
Were some you could choose,
For some served fine dinners
and some offered drinks and booze;
Then around the corner were Kaase's -
famous for chicken ala king
Or the Colonial Theater with stage shows was the thing.
Theaters were abounding -
the Orpheum, Strand, Keith Albee and Loew's
With first rate movies, music,
And some had exciting stage shows;
Portage Hotel had the Rubber Room -
An exciting place to be
For Akron was the Rubber City of the World -
Remembered in history;
The Merry-Go-Round Bar was an unusually fun place to be
Sometimes quite crowded with friends gathered
'round, like a family jamboree!
The Gareri Spaghetti House -
always crowded for all the good food,
With so much to choose from -
And all deliciously good;
Last, but not least, was the Mayflower Hotel
with bands and ballroom dancing
That made one feel they were in another world
so enchanting.
This was all just a few blocks in downtown Akron years ago
But it lives in our hearts as a wonderful place to know.

GOD'S WORLD

EARTH, SEA, AND SKY OF VARIED BLUES
AND STORMS AND RAINBOWS OF MYRIAD HUES
THIS IS GOD'S WORLD

TREES AND FLOWERS AND CARPETS OF GREEN
VALLEYS AND MOUNTAINS AND RIVERS SPARKLING CLEAN
THIS IS GOD'S WORLD

WILD ANIMALS AND EAGLES AND BIRDS ON THE WING
SNOWFLAKES LIKE CRYSTAL AND RAINDROPS OF SPRING
THIS IS GOD'S WORLD

THEN MAN LOOKED IT OVER AND SAID "THIS IS MINE
WITH BUILDINGS AND ROADS I CAN MAKE IT DIVINE"!
MAN AND HIS WORLD

SO ENCROACHMENTS AND GREED AND PLUNDER THAT RAVAGE
DESTROYING AND OVERPOWERING ALL THINGS LIKE A SAVAGE
HAVOC ON GOD'S WORLD

WE MUST NOW HEARKEN TO THE FINE GIFTS ON EARTH
AND RESTORE THINGS OF NATURE - DEARLY HELD IN GOD'S WORTH
GET BACK TO GOD'S WORLD

LET FOREST AND WILDLIFE AND CLEAN AIR PREVAIL
AND KEEP MODERN 'IMPROVEMENTS' DOWN TO PROPER SCALE
GET BACK TO GOD'S WORLD.

ERICA STUX

Erica Stux's life is one of many facets, not the least
of which is humor. Her writings have appeared in
many publications including
LOOK,
THE WALLSTREET JOURNAL,
GRIT,
THE PHILADELPHIA SUNDAY BULLETIN MAGAZINE,
AMERICAN LEGION MAGAZINE,
OUTDOOR WEST VIRGINIA,
POETRY PARADE
and a number of children's magazines
She grew up in Cincinnati and attended the University
of Cincinnati where she earned a master's degree in
chemistry. Since then she has followed a number of
vocations and avocations, being a chemist, technical
translator, housewife, mother, clubwoman, community worker.

Books she has written:
Jelly-Laughs and Chuckle-Lets
Landlady
Eight Who Made a Difference

JOHN BROWN'S HOME

I pass the house often,
White frame with columns on the porch,
Across the front yard a low stone wall
Of irregular shapes as though hastily piled up.

Tall fir trees on each side.
Feathery-leaved locusts towering over the roof,
A simple house, yet indispensable in its time.

I picture black figures approaching
On a moonless night
With frightened faces and thumping hearts.
A furtive knock on the back door,
Friendly hands reaching out.

"Come in, I'll fix you a plate of ham and beans.
You can stay out back in the hayloft.
Tomorrow night we'll guide you to the next safe house."

An oasis in a hostile world, a place of
Respite from the slings and scorpions
Of an obscene system.

He was a hero to many,
A fool and a madman to others,
Staunch and steadfast in his convictions.
A pity his misjudgments spelled disaster.

IT'S MAY
(On the Towpath Trail)

It's May;   I must get to the woods

Where willows lift gaunt branches to the sky,

And piebald sycamores conceal the oriole's blaze.

The trickling stream, diverted by the beaver's dike,

Has formed a lily-sprinkled marsh and placid pond

Where muskrats play and the prothonotary warbler

Preens, displaying golden head so dazzling,

It takes my breath away.

FOLLOW ME BACK TO AKRON
Song

Follow me back to Akron
The All-America city of ninety-five
Follow me back to Akron
The city that makes you feel happy to be alive.
Whoever comes to Akron
Will find a city that's really on the move
For polymer research a foremost base
It built an outstanding Inventure Place.
They're meeting the future with style and grace
in Akron.
There's the Soap Box Derby in August
And the Ohio Ballet
Theater productions to match those on Broadway
Beautiful metro parks and many lakes to fish
Golf and bowling matches,
Whatever sports you wish.
And there's Blossom Music Center
For symphonies, pop, or rock
Almost every summer evening
You'll find that's where thousands flock.
There's lovely Stan Hywet mansion
With tulips blooming in spring.
Killer whales and dolphins at Sea World's center ring
Canal days can be recalled when you take a hike
All along the Towpath
Or you can bring your bike.
Oh, follow me back to Akron
The place that's always meant the world to me.
Follow me back to Akron
You'll love it just like I do, wait and see
When you have lived in Akron as long as I have
Then you will agree
It's a city where everything's done with a flair
The spirit of progress hangs in the air.
There's no other city that can compare
With Akron.

BIOGRAPHY

Charles H. Tillson
Born on a farm 2 miles west
of Livermore, Iowa
February 29, 1920

Education:
Graduated High School
Livermore, Iowa - 1937

University Of Houston
Bachelor of Science
Mechanical Enigineering - 1950

Army Air Corps, !941 - 1945
Pilot - Instructor & Test Pilot

Professional Engineering Career
1950 thru 1995.

Married - Marie Petitt, June 12, 1943
Two Children
Timothy Ward Tillson, Born Aug. 18, 1952
Joan Marie Tillson, Born January 6, 1963
Marie Died, November 13, 1986.

Married - Alyce West, April 25, 1988

My poetic interest began after World. War II
I found that many of my mental concerns and
stresses were best alleviated if I wrote down
my thoughts and possible solutions often in
poetic form.

FAIRLAWN - TODAY AND YESTERDAY

Today Fairlawn is a city without a building tall,
And those who live there have the Summit mall,
And Towne Center provides many a diverse store,
A beauty salon, a barber shop, and a whole lot more.

T'is a suburban city dependent upon the family car,
For all the stores and shops are sited far,
From the homes of all who reside there,
In pleasant houses with lawns most fair.

It's a city where no railroad or river runs through,
Adjoined by commercial and industrial developments new,
There's Montrose, and farther up the street,
Many a restaurant for all who desire to meet and eat.

Yes, Fairlawn has with the passing of time a city become,
With all the amenities expected of one,
Exceptional schools, churches, and public parks,
Office and medical structures that now a city, marks.

To us, yesterday was the fall of nineteen sixty two,
And to the village of Fairlawn we were new,
Oh yes, the lawns there were green and fair,
And we were excited and happy to settle there.

Nearby were woods, a brook, and Fort Island park,
Where it was said the Erie Indians were made to depart,
Then there was the Fourth of July parade and on that day,
Children on bicycles led the parade on it's way.

And as the years rolled by and the village grew,
With many homes and businesses new,
Fairlawn did indeed a city become,
With all the advantages attributed to one.

MAPS AIR MUSEUM

There at CAK* on the airport west side,
MAPS Air Museum displays with great pride,
The legacy of America's aviation history.

There people of all ages come to see,
Military memorabilia and artifacts of what used to be,
And the tools of war beholden to our finest generation.

Museum members are proud to display,
Aircraft from long ago, and of a later day,
And tell the stories of how they served.

On the museum walls there reside great art,
And the artists are there who were a part,
Of the story that lies behind the paint.

The Louise Timken Aviation Research Library is a part,
Of the MAPS Air Museum where the young may start,
To learn that our history is the prophet of our future.

In the briefing room theater all may see,
The war films that describe much of our history,
And other films about flying and the life of a pilot.

Even more for all to enjoy are the collections,
Of aircraft restoration needs for the many sections,
Hand manufactured to make the planes whole once again.

There is a room filled with aircraft plastic models,
Where the visitors eyes will bug and ogle,
Over the collection that numbers a thousand or more.

The gift shop has many delights to prize,
Toys, kites, flight suits, shirts in any size,
And many other items promoting aviation and,
                    History.
            *CAK are the call letters for Akron-Canton
                Regional Airport

79

Considerations

I have read today of world affairs,
And I am greatly perturbed
I wonder why men must always at odds be,
When all are God's own, be they vassal or free.

We in America, Hebrew, Christian, all faiths.
Regard ourselves democratic and free, 'tis true,
But power and wealth have placed us in the fore,
As a leader of Nations. or even more.

What else is ours but to point the way,
That we have come oe'r ten score,
Tolerant of your neighbor living next door,
A proud heritage from those good men of yore.

Time was when the State was man's great concern,
And Nations were worlds apart.
But science has grouped us all, and I say,
That all the World is our neighbor today.

We are in time but hours away,
From the far corners of the earth, this we know,
Then who would deny a person, white, yellow, or black,
A thing we accept as mere matter-of-fact.
Freedom!

Yes, Freedom, Freedom to think as we please,
And choose freely our own society,
Accord all this privilege, and you shall see,
What a happy World God meant this to be.

Upon yourself take a close review,
Maybe you'll realize a thing or two,
That if upon others beliefs you do not encroach,
Why not to Nations apply this approach?

We are but mortals here upon this earth,
Imbued from childhood with certain beliefs.
Like Christians believing we are one with God,
Yet I can wonder about a divining God.

What of the Arab, Moslem, Hindu, or Jew,
Can you say that our God is not their's too?
For who shall ever know the extent of God's domain;
Or how many ways to worship him remain?

Yes, Christians are right in Christianhood,
But perhaps there are other ways also good,
For I have not the knowledge to deny,
That God on all his people may rely.

And so, where ever you may be,
Just lend a helping hand,
Then perhaps all shall find the way.
To God and peace, if we but one another.
Understand!

TOM TROYER

Taught school fourteen years - 1928 - 1943

Production Engineer - 1943 - 1957 -Fagal Products
(Twin Coach)

Realtor - 1957 - 1975 - Retired 1975

Long time member and past president of:
Akron Manuscript Club (the oldest writers club in Ohio)
Akron Area Poetry Society - since 1975

Founder and life member
Stow- Munroe Falls Chamber of Commerce

My wife of 66 years, Dorothea, and I were recognized
in 1980 as Stow's outstanding citizens.

Jaycee Distinguished Service award - 1977

WRITING A VILLANELLE

It's simple - take care that you don't blow it
Just call to mind a bit of repartee;
You needn't be a super duper poet.

If you are confused you shouldn't show it,
Then use your pen to write a line or three;
It's simple - take care that you don't blow it.

Doing well? You'll be the first to know it
When lines come easy and so fancy free
You needn't be a super duper poet.

In making rhyme it's apropos to show it
In feet and meter as it ought to be;
It's simple - take care that you don't blow it.

As you've reached the fifth with one to go, it
Spells out for you and then for me,
You needn't be a super duper poet.

Villanelle? You thought you couldn't do it,
But from your verse it's very plain to see
It's simple - take care that you don't blow it;
You needn't be a super duper poet.

THE BUM

We called him Irish Pat
He wore a broad brimmed felt
that shaded his ruddy face,
his corn cob pipe and
his bearded chin.

His hair was white as snow
hanging somewhat low on
the collar of his red and
black plaid coat he wore or
carried with him.

Pat walked like a sprightly elf.
It seemed to give an air of
charm to his bearing.
He always carried a cane although he
seldom used it.

Pat timed his visits well ,in
the second week in March just
before St. Patrick's Day, in
time for a farmer's breakfast of
ham and hotcakes.

As he ate he had stories to tell,
some true and some fabled.
We wondered about the
life he led before he
became a bum.

PALEFACE

We talk about the man in the moon,

But a woman must add to its light;

For no man would stay there all alone

And be out most every night.

THE SPIDER IN THE BATHTUB

It crawled up the slippery surface,

trying with all its might

to get out of its

white enameled prison;

only to fall back to the bottom

before reaching its freedom.

There to await its fate

in the dark reaches of the drain.

APOGEE

The richest

of men is

he who knows

the finest most

beautiful thoughts

to be those that

come from deep

in the heart of

Someone whose

message is

cloaked in

the fragrant

red rose.

86

IN NEED OF PRAYER

People rushing,
    getting nowhere;
Nations groping
    to no avail;
Each like a squirrel
    on a treadmill.

People live
    in glass houses,
Braced for the crash
    at any moment;
Then - a mountain
    of rubble.

This isn't the way
    it's intended
    but alas,
    so be it;
When we walk alone,
Not understanding
    that God is willing
    and waiting
    to help,
    when we ask
    for His guidance
    in prayer.

ROBERT ARDEN VAN KIRK (Bob)

Born: April 12, 1912
Graduate St. Martha's Grade School, North High School, attended Akron University and Notre Dame (summer school).
Worked at Akron YMCA State Boys Club division 1933-34-35.
Founded and was first director of CYO - Catholic Youth Organization 1942-46.
Founded and was director of Camp Santa Maria for Akron Knights of Columbus Council 547 - 1946-50.

Firestone Defense Products 1950-1977.

Beautification and summer youth director since 1980 for City of Munroe Falls.

In past years active in Boy Scouts, Soap Box Derbys, Elks, and past Grand Knight, Akron Knights of Columbus, Secretary of Akron K of C Building Company, etc.

Currently active in Akron and Stow Mens Garden Clubs, charter member and past president Cuyahoga Falls Mens Garden Club, member and past president Munroe Falls Historical Society, volunteer St. Thomas Hospital (Summa). Edit Falls Garden Club bulletin, the SEEDPOD.

Started writing a few verses in high school for opera singer star, my sister Mary Van Kirk. Have been writing ever since.

Married in 1936 to Geneva Twickler (deceased in 1984). We had two sons and two daughters. I have ten grandkids and nine great grandchildren.

OCTOBER OHIO

October in Ohio is a really gorgeous time,
Warmish days and tangy nights make a unique clime.
The landscape's a kaleidoscope of drops from nature's brush,
A startling panorama of rare colors lush.

October in Ohio brings a mystic clinging haze,
Filling all the dawnings with drifty misty blaze.
The air is very coolish until morning sunshine rays,
Evaporates fog's tendrils and light up the days.

October in Ohio means nut trees unload their wares,
Which squirrels and chipmunks gather for winter cares.
Now where gardeners garden there are flowers
a splendid sight
Mums in all their glory a-bloom with blossoms bright.

October in Ohio means ripe pumpkins in the fields,
And storage bins and silos filled with rich farm yields.
There is absolutely no where in this great land at all,
That can match living - in Ohio in the Fall.

THE PRO FOOTBALL HALL OF FAME

Canton's Pro Football of Fame,
Stands as monument to a game
That's vigorous and very rough,
All its contestants are quite tough,
For football is true physical go,
At all levels, especially pro.

Canton's Pro Football Hall of Fame
Honors special greats of the game,
Men selected from all the rest,
Chosen because they were the best,
Their achievements are recorded here,
Their records for each playing year.

Canton's Pro Football Hall of Fame
Is a show of love for this game,
Founded many long years ago
In this town of Canton, Ohio,
A visit here is to recall,
The wondrous world of pro football.

MUNROE FALLS TREE LIGHTING CEREMONY

This little pine tree is an emblem

Of a very special cause -

Planted to celebrate the yuletide,

For the folks of Munroe Falls.

It lifts its branches into the sky,

In front of the City Hall -

An expression of seasons greetings,

For our people one and all.

The tiny tree lights send a message,

Our twinkles are just for you -

May your family have a nice Christmas,

And all your wishes come true.

ALLEGORICALLY SPEAKING
MUNROE FALLS, OHIO, U.S.A. 1988

Lovely ladies and handsome men,
Seems a perfect phase to begin,
A few lines of written applause;
In speaking as I write this poem,
Of the little town I call home,
Here in Ohio - Munroe Falls.

This year of nineteen eighty eight,
We've had reason to celebrate,
And we have, in a proper way;
This torch now passes on to you,
In twenty thirty eight to do,
A party, proper to your day.

For each other and for our lands,
For our country, for what it stands,
Freedom for all our common cause;
It takes fortitude, one can't shirk,
To make our American way work,
We have this in our Munroe Falls.

VISIT STAN HYWET

There's an aura to Stan Hywet,
Which words cannot describe,
For the manor house and gardens,
Hold rare sights to imbibe.

All the many nooks and crannies,
Of the mansion and yards,
Blend in a surprise of vistas,
Like rhymes of ancient bards.

Here tiny buds are awaking,
There's big blooming flowers,
Here are viney aromas soft,
Lurking in green bowers.

Stan Hywet mirrors the old ways,
Reflecting much that's new,
Here a family loved and lived,
With dreams that ever grew.

As your eyes drink in the beauty,
That's just around each lee,
Breathe thanks to those who keep it,
For you and me to see.

LILA M. VAN SWERINGEN

Born December 7, 1927 in Cook, Nebraska, Mother Audrey Britt Marrs, Father George W. Marrs.
Husband Theodore Curtis Van Sweringen. Sons, Bryan T. Van Sweringen and Mark W. Van Sweringen. Divorced.

Published in Educational Secretarial Magazine, and the National Secretary Magazine, FALLS NEWS PRESS, CLEVELAND PLAIN DEALER, several anthologies of the National Library of Poetry, and Anderie Press, and received four Editor Choice Awards. A Distinguished Member of the International Society of Poets.

Attended Cook, Nebraska, and Waterville, Washington schools. Graduated Honorary Valedictorian. Attended Akron University, and correspondence courses from Notre Dame College for Women in Baltimore, Maryland.

Worked for U. S. War Department, U.S. Bureau of Reclamation, The Douglas County Auditor's Office in Washington state, and The Goodyear Tire & Rubber Company in Akron, Ohio.

Served as President of the Richardson Elementary PTA, Cuyahoga Falls. Retired Staff Member Emeritus of Cuyahoga Falls Board of Education as Administrative Assistant to the Superintendent.

Co-Founder of the Ohio Chapter of the National Educational Office Professionals. President, named Outstanding Educational Office Employee of the Year by the Ohio Chapter in 1980-1981. The chapter underwrites a thousand dollar scholarship annually named the Lila M. Van Sweringen Student Scholarship for an Ohio high school senior in public or private schools.

A member of the First United Methodist Church of Cuyahoga Falls. Served as teach in toddler class, member of handbell choir, Chancel Choir, accompanist for childrer choirs, kindergarten bible school teacher preparing coloring book artwork for the school.. A member of the Tire Town Chapter of the International Administrative Assistants Association, the Friends of Taylor-Memorial Library, associate member the Cuyahoga Falls School Foundation. Trustee of Civic Music Association. Serve on Speaker's bureau for business classes at high schools in the area.

Philosophy of Poetry: Life is made of major and minor chords which poetry blends into harmony of life.

SMOKESTACKS

We rolled into town on railroad tracks to Mill Street Station,
I had never been to Akron, the Rubber Capital of the nation.
However, when I saw the dismal, dark train terminal there
I wondered why I had decided to make my life here.

The prospective in-laws met my fiance' and me at the time
And all seemed very pleasant and sublime.
As we headed south toward the Greensburg direction
I never saw so many smokestacks belching smoke in all directions.

I made the comment that these were so ugly and unappealing
And my to be mother-in-law's remark left me reeling.
"Never say anything about the smoke from them as this means work."
And in the Rubber Capital they had known Depression at its worst.

Being from the rural area of the Mid-West, I had never realized
Some folks were in the East living through what I had not surmized.
Although we were poor, too, we had the garden and food to eat
Cows to give milk, and pork and beef for meat.

I was sorry I mentioned the deplorable smokestacks then
I didn't realize what had happened so many years ago to them.
Now the rubber companies have moved the construction away
And no more smokestacks, just Headquarters here to stay.

I am thankful for the time that I knew the countryside
Where there was no smoke nor industry did not abide.
However, I can relate to those who felt oppression
When homes were lost, and jobs through the Depression.

THE GOODYEAR FAMILY

I was fortunate to be employed by Goodyear
And had a position which I enjoyed year after year.
Being a part of a department planning stores
Was so exciting to see where they were built and more.

Even in Beirut, Lebanon, a land so far away
Where tire was spelled 'tyre' - and Goodyear there to stay.
Years later when the bombing of the Marines happened there
I thought of my happy days at Goodyear planning the store there.

They tell me now that Goodyear is not as it used to be
When Eddie Thomas and Paul Litchfield made it family.
I was a very fortunate individual to be a part
Of a tire company which built tires and stores from the heart.

Now, the Goodyear Global Headquarters are here
The construction of tires as I knew are gone everywhere..
It was seven years I was part of a department association
That gave one the joy of being in that wonderful profession.

HARVEY FIRESTONE

There is a statue of Harvey Firestone
Setting on a chair made of stone.
Overseeing the factory he founded years ago
And made work for families here to grow.

The Harbel Manor House has been torn down
And there are condominiums built all around
It seems such a waste for a lovely home
To have been destroyed and forgotten by some.

I am sure that the folks living in condos there
May not remember the lovely home of yesteryear.
However, as I survey Harvey's statue on South Main
I sometimes wonder if he feels the loss and the pain.

THE CANAL LOCKS

One can hardly remember when years ago these canals were made
To help transport the coming and going of the tire trade.
However, today, though not used for that connection
The area has been groomed to become an attraction.

Canal Park as it is now become known
Is a lovely place for folks to roam.
Also, the ball diamond that has been built there
Afford folks the opportunity to enjoy games with families to share.

Although time changes the faces of a location
One realizes that it still is the best of a nation
For Canal Locks to be a part of the heart of Akron
Truly, this is an important triumphant faction.

97

STAN HYWET

Frank and C. W. Seiberling founded the Goodyear Tire
And in doing so there were many men to hire.
Frank A. planned a home for him and his family
And it has become a place in history.

For those who tour the gardens and house area
Can never find any place more delightful to see
From mums in Fall, to the Christmas decorations
To tulips in Spring, and roses in Summer locations.

The Carriage House has hosted many celebrations
Of weddings and anniversaries, and other occasions.
Although the family does not abide there anymore
The memories and the love will remain forevermore.

So Stan Hywet is a lovely place to visit and see
Something that will live on in history.
All who will tour the home and grounds now and forever
Will realize the home and gardens will never sever.

READER'S DIGEST BEST

Many years ago in a Reader's Digest edition
Listed a town as one of the 24 best in the nation.
Located on the banks of the Little Cuyahoga River of renown
Cuyahoga Falls, Ohio, is the name of this town.

When I left my home in the Far West -
Which I thought was the best place to rest
I found that this town of Cuyahoga Falls
Had come to be one of the best of Eastern halls.

We bought our first home here in 1952
A bungalow in what was called "Heslop's Hatchery" to quite a few.
For here the World War II Veterans had come to buy
And to live and work and raise families close by.

Now as the years have gone fleetingly by
I have had the pleasure of being a resident without a try.
Our sons attended the schools here in the 24th best town
in the nation.
And, I, too, worked with the schools in education.

The end of the century is drawing nigh
And the year of 2000 will find me still high
On the best of the East instead of the West
And have found Cuyahoga Falls my retirement home to rest.

THE POWER HOUSE ON THE RIVER

It is such a lovely thing to do -
Go out to lunch or dinner in a renovated power house, too.
You can dine and view the old pieces above and below
And view the Cuyahoga River and the Falls, a real show.

To go back in time and take such a power station
And turn it into something to make this a lovelier location.
The bricks and stone and mortar which turned on power
Now provide many people with lovely lunch and dinner hours.

Watch the ducks on the river below
And the possum catching fish for his dinner in tow.
It is hard to believe that we are nearing
Century 20
When we sit in a place where dreams were realized plenty.

THE RIVERFRONT MALL

Come with me to the Riverfront Mall
There we will really have a ball.
From the Irish-American festivals galore
And the Lions Club Rib Burn-Off, Oktoberfest, and more.

Families gather here to leisurely stroll
Along the Mall and greet folks they know.
The Cuyahoga River runs along the way
And truly makes for a lovely, lovely day.

Take a ride on the pontoon boat
And go under bridges to the wetlands remote.
See where the Indians of yesteryear swam years ago
And hear the history told to us as we slowly go.

THE THURSDAY LUNCH SERENADE

Come with me to the Thursday Lunch Serenade
Have a burger, or hot dog, with the best sundae made.
For you can avail yourself of Riverside Sweets
The restaurant with the best of soups and meats.

While the band plays across the way
On a very lovely summer's day
You can eat and tap your foot with glee
And then fill up on an ice cream sundae.

The bands that come to serenade you
Play jazz, and tunes that make you happy and blue.
For many of the tunes will bring back memories
Of the times long, long ago of friends and sweeties.

So on Thursday from noon until two
All through the summer months true
The Riverfront Centre Mall will provide
Food and tunes that will make you glad you did imbibe.

THE ARBORETUM

Mr. Carl Graefe had a lovely dream
To plant an arboretum of trees across from a stream,
An underground spring filled the pond below the land
And truly, a lovelier place could not be planned.

However, the dream did not become a reality
Instead, it became the Chestnut Hill Memorial Cemetery.
Here the dogwoods and azaleas bloom in the spring
And leaves turned to color in the fall mirror the pond
Which now houses a fountain and sometimes rainbows abound..

The ducks, geese, and swans glide over the pond
And people come from miles around
To show their children the lovely area there
And feed the ducks with lettuce, and other fare.

Although the dream did not become an arboretum as planned
It truly is a beautiful landscape with pond as a band,
Daffodils, tulips, and other bulbs have been planted
And cared for by the caretaker of the cemetery and groomed,
Not only bodies of loved ones passed away are so entombed.

So, if you have a time some lovely day -
Whether in the fall, or the spring, or on a summer way
The beauty of the arboretum once planned
Still is a breathtaking spot for trees planted by God and man.

And the loved ones who are buried there
Have souls that have gone to be in God's care,
The beauty of a final resting place
Must be the hand of God's blessing with His grace.

CHRISTOPHER'S

If you do not care to go to a restaurant and dine alone
There is just a place for you that is well known.
It is called CHRISTOPHER'S BISTRO on Portage Trail
And eating there will provide friendship and more to avail.

For Chris who is the Chef in the kitchen there
Prepares food with a real taste and unusual flair
From the fried chicken and pastas galore
And the salads, and chicken wings, you will want more.

Bobbie, the maitre de is Chris's Mom, you see
And she is such a friendly, pleasant little sweetie.
As you dine at lunch, or dinner, or breakfast fare
I am sure you will find you are never alone there.

After church services it is a real treat
To have breakfast at CHRISTOPHER'S BISTRO,
a fine place to eat
And maybe, someday, the deli will become a reality
And Chris will bake cinnamon rolls that are heavenly.

BLOSSOM

Come with me to the rolling hills and vales
And sit with me in a lovely pavillion or on the lawn
To hear the music of all composers of renown
And be out in God's world surrounded by beautiful sound.

When the Fourth of July comes it is fun
To pack a picnic lunch and go with everyone
To listen to the marches of John Phillip Sousa
And clap hands and laugh and enjoy a birthday by tuba.

When the fireworks light up the sky on the Fourth
You know that you are in an area where life really comes forth.
Blossom Music Center in Cuyahoga Falls location
Is truly a lovely spot to listen to man's musical creation.

THE PORTHOUSE THEATER

Near Blossom, this amphitheater sets
In a green space framed with trees of all sects.
The season opens in the summer time.
And, all kinds of plays, serious, fun and sublime.

When Shakespeare beckons with MIDSUMMER NIGHT'S DREAM
Many, many folks, will be seated awaiting this play supreme.
It is only natural that the plays be held here
For everyone to come from far and near.

We have a CAMELOT right in our location
And the performance of players proves this creation.
If you enjoy PUMP BOYS AND DINETTES on the onset of series
You will enjoy all of the wonderful plays presented tastefully.

If you would like to have something to drink and eat
There is a wonderful setting for a picnic treat
Tables are arranged not too far away
Where one can eat either on or before the evening or show matinee.

So do plan to attend PORTHOUSE THEATER plays
These will make for the end of lovely summer days.
The antics held on the lawn before the presentation
Will delight all young and old like a celebration.

THE CUYAHOGA VALLEY NATIONAL PARK

A world of beauty is just a few miles to the north
Of forests, and glades, and rocks, and brooks brought forth
By God when He made the land in the area around us
Has brought more than just vision and love of forest.

The Towpath has been built by man to lend place
For those who enjoy a walk or jog at any pace.
The beauty as they go on their way
Brings joy to all and appreciation of their stay.

We are grateful to the political powers that be
Who saw to it that this land would not be disturbed for you and me.
The Cuyahoga Valley National Park has become
Well known not just to us living here but others who come.

So never leave this area without taking the time
To see the park which lends to beauty and is sublime
I am thankful that this land of glades, rocks, and brooks
Will always go down in all history and other books.

JONATHAN HALE HOMESTEAD

Further East a young man courted his bride-to-be
And told her he would build a mansion for her and their family.
So the Hale Homestead began here in the Western Reserve
And the bricks made here to build the home to serve.

As the family grew, so did the mansions walls
And there were many, many more families in the halls.
Nearby there was a cemetery location
For those of the Hale family who left to Heaven's destination.

The Homestead has been turned into a very historical place
With maple sugar made there in March with oxen treading at a
slow pace.
The home hosts a lovely Wassail Bowl at holiday time
And folks dress in the clothing of the historical time.

As the Western Reserve Historical Society grew
So did the Hale Homestead part grow, too.
Salt box houses were brought here to set
And further renovation of how things were for Hale kept.

When people come for a vacation in this spot
They must go to the Hale Homestead to see what was the lot
For a man and his wife to come from East to West to live
And raise families and start a historical reserve dedicated
to the times they lived.

THE MUSEUM OF FASHION

If you would like to see fashion designs of the century
Do plan to take a trip to Fashion Museum of Kent State University.
For there under the direction of the Dean of Arts
You will see fashion from our country and world from all parts.

Queen Victoria's lingerie was there at one time on display
Can you imagine such a tiny little one ruling England far away?
There have been beautiful robes made from silk and brocades
That adorned the rulers of Japan for many decades.

All of the mannequins have hair made of paper curls
It is unbelieveable how lifelike these displays are of girls,
There are gowns and beautiful cloaks which had trains trailed
On the stars of Hollywood and Broadway each described and detailed.

The quilt displays which have been in the museum from long ago
And those made today make such a lovely, beautiful show,
Also, there are items made from glass and materials to see
Such a wonderul museum so different at the University.

Do plan to go to Kent State University in Kent, Ohio
To see an unusual fashion museum promoting the world so,
The building housing this museum is beautiful to see
And truly promotes the world of the fashion industry.

Students taking the coursework of fashion and designs
Most certainly have an opportunity to enrich their minds.
With the on-site display of fashion from days gone by
To plan for the fashion for days as a new century draws nigh.

MOLLY'S TEA ROOM

Come with me to Medina and you will see -
The most lovely place designed for lunch and tea.
The young woman who designed and planned this place
Had a mother who lost in the breast cancer race.

Therefore, the owner, took money she received from the estate
And made something original, and yet helped to solve the cancer race.
For ever so many times, the money made at the room
Goes to the Cancer Research to stop this disease boom.

The elegant Victorian decor of the rooms abound
And the delicious cuisine is truly the best around.
From scones, to lemon tea bread, and the flavored teas
To flavored coffees, and delicious desserts that do tease.

My favorite is the Chicken Divan - which is so Divine
And served with the cranberry salad and raspberry tea so sublime.
So do plan to travel to Medina some day soon
And dine in pleasure and beauty in Miss Molly's Tea Room.

PUBLIC SQUARE

Remember many years ago when
There were many stores in Public Square in Cleveland then
Higbees, and Halles, and May Company and many more
Bringing high fashion and tea rooms to the Square galore.

Today there is a lovely Renaissance Hotel
Which overlooks Public Square and cars going pell mell.
The statue of Moses Cleveland stands in this Square
And pigeons roost there and you know what everywhere.

However, it is still a fun place to go
And, we do miss the stores of long ago
Time changes the City of Cleveland and others
But, still in Public Square, we are all sisters and brothers.

THE BROWNS AND THE INDIANS

Never did I show interest in professional football
Until I came to Cleveland found in Kosar it was all.
I will have to admit that when the Browns left town
I, too, felt badly for the crowd of the Dog Pound.

However, all is joy in Cleveland now
For the Browns are back and will play football and how.
The Cleveland Indians still are in town
And they brought home the American League Crown.

However, my wish is this - and from the heart
That with all sport stadiums there must be a part
For more consideration given to the ailing schools
After all, education is what should be the main tools.

A city as large as Cleveland is now
With Cleveland Clinic and University Hospitals avow
That there is good in promoting the best in health plans
But with the schools in such disarray
It takes Glamour of Browns and Indians in my heart away.

THE CLEVELAND FLATS

I had never known of the Cleveland Flats
Could not imagine where these were at.
However, some years I came to know
Where there was fun and great places to go.

The STAR OF NAUTICA sailed on the Cuyahoga River
And out to Lake Erie for a lovely view to deliver.
Lunch in the dining room on the deck below
And up to top deck to see Cleveland Skyline while in tow.

Now I know where the Cleveland Flats are
And I have enjoyed going and tasting the "caviar."
For this is an awakening to me
Of how great this area can be.

THE SALT OF THE LAKE

Did you know that Lake Erie covers a bed of salt?
This is mined with covered culverts like a vault.
An interesting fact that I never knew
Until I saw a TV show telling of this in review.

I don't know where the salt mined goes
Probably, on many roads when covered with snows.
However, it is still a mystery to me.
How there can be a bed of salt below Lake Erie.

111

THE FABULOUS VANS

James Tower Van Sweringen was his name
A poor man to Wooster with sons who would rise to fame.
The boys, Oris and Mantis attended a one room school house
Near Doylestown, to learn lessons for business to espouse.

Eventually they went to Cleveland, a big town
And were newspaper boys on the streets to build renown.
One had the vision and dream, and one the know-how
To plan and build with monies borrowed for dreams, not a plow.

Shaker Heights was a town laid out by their plan
With land for schools so education would be at hand.
The town was too far from the Cleveland downtown
And a transit system had to be found.

So the boys borrowed more money to buy railroad land
And thus enabled the Rapid Transit to downtown Cleveland ran.
The Terminal Tower, a skyscraper of renown
Was built by Oris and Mantis in Public Square of Cleveland town

The day of the opening of the beautiful tower
Served a luncheon for twenty five hundred to devour.
However, the boys did not attend the feted event there
They decided to spend the time in the Penthouse away from the far

Later on they built homes for them and their sisters nearby
These were side by side in Shaker Heights beautiful countryside.
Then it was time for a mansion to be planned to build
And it was located in Gates Mills and called "Daisy Hill."

THE FABULOUS VANS (Con't)

The business ventures grew and were involved with not a few
Plans continued to be made and more dreams realized
But, never the dream that not all would survive.
The Depression of the thirties came and the end was in view.

The Van's fortunes and those of many others became lame,
In order to save the empire they had planned
They invested their personal fortune to save this demand.
They did not live to see TOWER CITY, what a pity.

"Daisy Hill" was sold for taxes at a later date
And early deaths for both the boys were their fate.
However, it cannot be denied two farm boys
Lived to envision worthwhile dreams fruition and bring joys.

They are buried with the Rockefellers in the Cemetery of Lakeside
And there the visions and dream boys are buried side by side.
But the memories of their ventures and dreams a reality
Are proven by Shaker Heights, and Terminal Tower, beautifully.

FIRST TIME FOURTH TERM

I have had the pleasure to see - a fourth term mayor in our vicinity
The first time the candidate entered the mayoral race you see
He lost, but this did not quell his determination
To sometime win the Mayoral Race in the Cuyahoga Falls election.

It has been my opportunity to know this Mayor from his first bid
For the Mayoral Race and it was like springtime when entered
His enthusiasm and exhuberance had never quavered
And a win for the Mayoral Race was something he savored.

And so he worked, and very hard indeed
Using experience from the Marines, and Firestone speed.
He entered the Council race and won
And proved to all here was a young man, hometown's son.

He won the Mayoral Race and proved to all
That he had the best interest of Cuyahoga Falls on the ball.
Northampton Township annexed to the Falls he planned
And this happened and provided much more land.

The Sheraton Suites came into being on the River
And the beauty of the place made one quiver.
Although he took plenty of flack from many folks
He had enough confidence in his plans to win votes.

Now today we have a fine, young man, hometown grown
Who has provided Cuyahoga Falls with one of its own.
A distinguished alumnus of Cuyahoga Falls High awarded
And, truly, one which all felt he deserved being rewarded.

Then, the FIRST TIME - fourth term mayor he became
And Don L. Robart is his name.
He has led our town to a place of fine reputation
In many fields of recycling, schools, and citizen recreation.

So - I am proud to say that I was one
Knowing Don when he started out for a Mayoral Race and WON.
He is a hard worker who never shirks from his duty
And has helped to make Cuyahoga Falls, a fine city.

IRWIN T. WHITE

Irwin T. White graduated from the University of
Wyoming with a BS in Mechanical Engineering.

Sales engineering career in Chicago, Indianapolis,
Buffalo, Detroit, and back to Cleveland office, later
became vice president of company.

Started writing poetry in college
and has kept writing since, including Christmas cards.

Writes poems and sonnets for special events.

Present writing entitled THE BIBLE FOR DUMMIES -
Old Testament verses reworked into rhyming couplets.
To date, has finished eight books of the Bible.

OUR TOWN

Shady streets

Quiet retreats

Gardens fair

Waiting there.

Hollyhocks

In dainty frocks

Of red and white

A bee's delight.

A languid breeze

And lazy trees

Your troubles await

To dissipate.

HOLLYHOCKS

Sing of your old oaken bucket
Of the cool moss-covered well,
Of woodland trees and a sighing breeze
And your hideaway mountain dell.
But my song is another tune,
Of something that delights the eyes,
Of a magic look in the picture book
In which nature paints and dyes.
For I sing:
Of hollyhocks in our alleys,
Hollyhocks bordering the streets,
Hollyhocks in bloom under a full moon,
Hollyhocks defying the heat.
Hollyhocks on stems tall and slender,
Prim as an old fashion maid,
A colorful bloom to brighten the gloom
When summer's memories shall fade.

APRIL SNOW

(N. E. Ohio averages 2 - 6 inches of snow in April)

You have no right to touch the ground,
To make a person look and frown
At nature's whim which does let fly
December snow from April sky.

You flutter down without a sound,
Transient beings to world spring bound.
Your silent noise is as a sigh,
A rattle of death before you die.

There's scarce enough to make a mound
Before the sun comes swinging round
And makes of winter's futile try
A damp and muddy, misty lie.